There Is a Doe in the Winter Hayfield

There Is a Doe
in the Winter Hayfield

a poem by
Susan Gordon

Concrete Wolf
Chapbook Award Series

Copyright © 2016 Susan Gordon

ISBN 978-0-9964754-3-3

Design: Tonya Namura using
Simplifica (display) and Cochin (text)

Cover photo: Susan Gordon
Author photo: Shannon Seymour,
Three Hearts Photography

Concrete Wolf Poetry Chapbook Series
Concrete Wolf
PO Box 445
Tillamook, OR 97141

http://ConcreteWolf.com
ConcreteWolfPress@gmail.com

This book is dedicated to my two daughters,
Elizabeth Ker Gordon and Miriam Cela Gordon,
who have always shown me the way.

Contents

3
There Is a Doe in the Winter Hayfield

27
Epilogue

29
Acknowledgements

31
About the Author

There Is a Doe
in the Winter Hayfield

I have been hearing the exploding cracks
of rifle shots from the long, empty farm behind mine

I don't know those hunters
but I know their signs
I find molasses and corn in August
left out to call the velvet-antlered buck into ambush
I find beer cans and orange peels
as the raw dark of hunting season sets in

There is a doe in the winter hay field

I allow a hunter here, Nick
a bow-hunter, quiet, waiting
quick to follow if he has wounded

He has never left a deer behind

There is a doe in the winter hay field

Belly shot
she died running
her legs outstretched
stilled mid-gallop
She died in extremity
in flight

There is a doe in the winter hay field

She is close to whole
her skyward eye plucked
one ear torn
Other than that, she is
a sweet-faced beauty
with a long white throat and a dark nose

There is a doe in the winter hay field

And today
something has started
eating her
Her tail is gone
just an edge of hip bone shows
ivory white
against the browning orchard grass

I talk to my hunter, Nick, and he says
Fox and coyote will eat a deer like that

There is a doe in the winter hay field

Nick asks, *Do you want me to drag her
out of the field to the edge of the woods?*

Quick I answer
No, I am keeping her company

I recognize the truth
I am keeping her company
I am visiting her day by day
marking her transformation
from fur to flesh to bone

There is a doe in the winter hay field

Slowly she is being eaten
No part of her is wasted
hide, innards, flesh
hips, haunches, belly
Yesterday I saw some small rib bones

her twisted spine
a jagged row of gapped, unclaimed teeth

There is a doe in the winter hay field

Today the River dog and I are coming
from the woods two fields away
and I wonder what dark man is
standing beyond my pines

I hush River
and pull him closer
Suddenly the silent man spreads great wings
and lifts lazy into the air

This bird, this black robed priest
This is my body
This is my blood
These are my bones

There is a doe in the winter hay field

She is herself
She is every hurt thing

I visit her day after day
a witness, a student
of my fields, my woods
of the silent bone clatter
of unraveling
of what comes
after everything has been undone

There is a doe in the winter hay field

Today I walk
muffled
except for the sharp snap of a stick
through the stand of pines
and shush, shush, shush
through sodden grass

The doe has transformed again
Her hide has been pulled
back away from her ribs
Three of those long bones
are cracked off
splintered stumps

What takes my breath
is all the blood

She is two weeks dead
and half-eaten

But there it is
pooled, wine-red
in her chest cavity

The rain is coming steady
each drop into her body
raises
a tiny ruby crown

that leaps up

then falls
leaving ring after ring after ring
in that dark pond

Small beauty

It is because of her
that I go to Christmas Eve Mass

Cold, ripped, wet
she makes me ask of the Eucharist
What is being offered?
What is being taken in?

I find no answers in the service

I do not hold the doe
in me
as I quickly dip
a dry thin wafer
into the chalice of wine

Christmas morning breaks
clear and sunny
I take my short walk
beneath the pines
into the hay field

She is changed again

The fur has dried about her neck
Something has pierced her
and eaten her heart

There now, I say to her, *you have died*

We have both been waiting for this

Yesterday's dark chilling rain
so hard on her body
This loss of her heart
is some kind of birth

Mid-afternoon
River dog and I take a walk
in the fields that she had fled
Not to be shot ourselves
we are dressed in orange

As we leave those fields
cross through my woods
I see black kites
turkey vultures
above her body
at play

The wind is up
They are riding currents
dipping together
soaring apart

Day by day
I keep her company

So little flesh
so little substance
whatever is eating her
is chivvying her around

No longer does she hold
the same piece of ground

When I look for her each morning
she is a smaller tan hump

And

She is more and more bone
I can see how deep her chest was
how those long rib bones were made
to protect lungs and heart

I can see the length and strength of her leg bones
hip to patella
how she was built
to pull in a long breath and run

There is a doe in the winter hay field

Today
everything is rent again
There is no forgiveness in dying

Her hide is pierced
her legs a running jumble
her brain has been taken

I no longer know what to make of this

There is no holiness
no larger meaning
just duty
me to her
her to me

There is a doe in the winter hay field

She is
a sodden sacrifice

her legs a tangle
of half-eaten bones

Her scapula has been
pulled free, lies
a bone kite
red and white
on withered grass

Still, even in the
cold grey sleet
her face is serene

She is herself
She feeds the birds, the fox,
the coyote, the neighbor's dog
She feeds me
although I drag my feet
now
when I come to her altar

There is a doe in the winter hay field

This morning

fifteen years
after my mother's death
I walk out

on a cold grey
day
to see
the doe

There is a breath of snow
on the ground
and more coming

She has taken
yet another shape

Her rib bones
are desolate
her face
a shimmer
of white

She is
at a masked ball
dark-eyed
with a tender gaze
The inch of crystals
returning to her
an open mouth
a quivering nose

If it weren't for
her cracked bones
jutting up
her broken pelvis
she would rise up and dance

There is a doe in the winter hay field

Tonight
pulling into my lane
at 9:00 o'clock
I startle
a large doe
lipping black oil sunflower seed
from my open bird feeder

She trots
across the yard
looking over
her shoulder
calling
without a sound

And suddenly
a September fawn
sheltering
behind the rhododendron
next to the screened-in porch
dashes over grass and gravel
to join his mother

There
I think
Life again

There is a doe in the winter hay field

1 to 3 was predicted
and frozen rain

What comes is 10 inches
of hard-driven snow
then late night sleet

a frozen glaze
over everything

This afternoon
each footstep
breaking through
the sharp crust
I set out
to find her

I thought she
would be buried
just another white mound

But
there she is
turned over once again
a shock of fawn and white
Caught in the froth of fur
one slender brown leg
one black ballerina hoof

Just when I think
she is nothing
but shattered bones
just when I think
I know who she is
she shakes me

Look again
Look again

There is a doe in the winter hay field

Today the last late snow
is melting quick
I can see
in receding white
and widening brown
the steps I took to her
when the snow
was eighteen inches deep

I knew my way
orienting on the boundary tree
and my memory
of her garbled spine
and scattered legs

But that day
she was hidden
not even a lift
or a curve
to mark her place

Now I see
I had come just to her

I am astonished
and
not at all surprised
I could have
reached out
and touched
her single hoof
with my booted toe

There is a doe in the hayfield

She is all high ribs
her hide looped around them
but her spine is missing
so are her hind legs

I can't imagine what carried them off

Her skeletal neck and bone face
are still attached
They are against the ground
She is flipped onto her back

The arc of mangled bones
looks like it might rise
into the air

I didn't know it would be like this

I had somehow imagined her
going from flesh to bone
but now half of her has vanished

I walk round and round her
There is a radiance of ribs
seen anew
because they are all that is

If I could step within
I would find myself
in a king's hall, a cathedral

But when I step back
she is the great keel
of a slowly listing ship

How many times did
I walk around her?
After some inward nod
some reconciliation
I walk back towards the house
and come upon
one scapula, one foreleg, one hoof

Then I turn to my left and see
stretched out
still running
her spine and two hind legs

They had been there for weeks
It is the ribs and neck and face

wrenched free and set afloat

She is a trinity

For now, this moment

Until the next

There is a doe in the hayfield

Today, I take a pound and a half
of good Angus ground beef out to the doe

I break it into rounds of three
one for the place where her ribs, neck and head lie
one for her spine, the fan spread of her hind legs
one for a single front leg, scapula and black hoof

We are halfway into Holy Week
and this is the best I can do

a simple offering
to the ones who have been stripping her
of fur and hide, bone and flesh

a bow
to dog, fox, coyote,
vulture, crow and kite
a kind of communion

a prayer on behalf of the doe
from the holy in me to the holy in them

There is a doe in the hayfield

Friday morning, the day of the Crucifixion
I walk out to see the doe
The hamburger has vanished

The whole of the year has felt
like a crucifixion:
four hard deaths
and the doe
some kind of tapestry

I begin looking up services
at the Episcopal churches in town

Transfiguration has a noon service
I can just make it there in time

The whole church is the color of light oak
The altar is oak
so are the railings, the pews, the wooden cross

As I pray I can feel my hand reaching out
to touch the doe

I cannot seem to take Communion
with any reverence
I feel pushed and quick
I cannot be present in this small moment

But what I am left with is gift enough

Touch her

Home, I go about the small chores I set for myself
I take the unused wood from the house to the woodpile
I trim low branches from still bare trees
I go out to see the doe
the three she has become

Her skull, neck and ribs lie close to the ground

For the first time
I reach out and stroke her

The crest of her ribs is bleached white
silky to my touch
smooth and sun-warmed
but cooling now, in the early evening

Underneath they are
furred and rough like a cat's prickly tongue

This touch, this prayer
answer to her long supplication

I come home
pull River's dog blanket outside
and lie down watching birds in the maple
listening to the growl of the wind

There are so many birds
the tree is trembling
There are pale brown and purple doves
goldfinches, male and female marked just alike
the male in yellow and black
the female in beiges and browns
tufted titmice
black and white flickers
the grey-blue nuthatch
and black-capped chickadees

If I sigh they flutter

There is a bit of time
when no bird moves
I see a small hawk fly above me

As he sails beyond Whiskey Creek
the birds begin to stir and eat again
before the darkness comes

Easter Sunday
I walk out to her
noticing
how
all of a sudden
the orchard grass is greening

how
all of a sudden
the clover is around her bone face
and
yards away
is pushing up between
the lacy gaps of her isinglass spine

As I walk away
the little birds come
light along her ribs
pecking at her bones
to strengthen
the shells of the eggs
they will lay

There is a doe in the hay field

It is coming close to haying time

I do as I promised
I call Donna's phone
and when she doesn't answer
I call Jason's
then Donna again

There is doe in the hayfield, I say
Her skull, ribs, neck and spine
I am worried she'll
break the mowing blade
tangle the rake

Don't worry, says Donna
Jason will get her

And I think to myself
No, he won't
I will

I roll down my sleeves
pull on my yellow deerskin gloves
the ones I wear
when I am messing with thorns
poison sumac or poison ivy

I march through my pines
into the orchard grass
that comes to my waist
down
then up
keeping my eye on the boundary tree
watching for a lower run of grass
where Nolan ran the semi last fall

The blue green hay
becomes shorter clover
I know I am near
Still it takes some searching
before I find her

I slip my left gloved hand
between her ribs
and pull her up
She is lighter than I imagined

With my right hand
I pick up her front leg
and scapula
and fold it
switch blade neat

Walking this way
through thigh-high hay
breaking a track
she hangs from my curled fingers
her head low, a bone drum
slicing through high grass

I come just into the woods

I had thought of laying her
in the patch of sumac
behind the half-downed
cherry tree
the place
where I found
the bones of a buck
two years ago

But as I enter the woods
I look to my right
there is a long-fallen tree
split
soft copper belly dust
entering the earth

There, I think, *there*

I leave the path
careful to step over
the reaching poison sumac
and lay her down
in that fox-red
sponge of
tree innards

Because I hadn't cradled her
she has swiveled
The hide rope has turned
to the last of the fawn and white fur
and her head lines out stiff
not touching the ground

I take the jackknife
of folded leg and scapula
and lay it next to her

She is home with
other faltering things
a massive tree
becoming a thick run of sweet earth
a place where I will pass her
day by day
season by season
as I move from my land
to the ill-used farm beyond

I turn and trace my tracks
through the hay
line up with the lone tree
the semi track
and begin looking for her spine and hind legs

I go round and round
I tread fine grass and clover
Circle upon circle
marks my path

I cannot find that other portion of her

There is a doe

The hayfields have been shorn
I walk through the stubble
my feet, crabs skittering along
scratching cracked dirt

I am looking for the whirligig
the hula-hoop of her spine and
hind legs

But they are gone
vanished
as if she had never been

Curved spine
long legs
femur, thigh bone
patella, cannon bone
and two delicate pointed black hoofs

Gone

I warned Jason
to look for them
when his hired men cut the hay

He said they never saw them

Was there a midnight crescent moon
that lit the way
as she pirouetted
en pointe
from this piece of land?

I cannot say

her last clattering bones
appear to have taken flight

and I have scoured
the hard ground
waiting for rain

Epilogue

When I first saw the deer, she was a beautiful fawn and white doe, sweet faced, belly shot. Six months later, she was no more than a skull, spine, ribs, and one foreleg that I rescued from a field about to be hayed. I layed these few bones at the beginning of the woods in the orange dust of a downed, decaying tree.

The doe came and I will say that again, she came, and there is the gift. She held me in the moment; there was no escaping where I was, where she was, each day. This leaning into death and dismemberment was teaching me.

My life has been marked by so many deaths: my father when I was 14; my Aunt Jean when I was 18; my Aunt Nancy and Grandpa when I was 32; my husband, Ralph, when I was 51; my mother when I was 52; and my daughter, Liz, when I was 60. I hate death; it is the enemy. But the doe came and I was drawn to her every morning, month by month as she transformed again and yet, again. So many of my people were cremated; we had no truck with long decay. With the doe, what we had hidden, I now watched. She came and I wrote, a poem for every visit until, in the end, I had poems enough for a little book.

Acknowledgments

This small book, There Is a Doe In The Winter Hayfield, would not have come into being without the steady support of three people. My gratitude for their presence in my life knows no bounds.

Max Regan has been my writing teacher and mentor since my daughter, Liz's, death in 2007. What I have learned and relearned from him is to walk into the hardest places and to not veer away. I also learned that deep grief is not the only thing, that joy remains. Max taught me to write fearlessly and with abandon, to never denigrate the "messy first draft," but to learn that it always holds the soul of the final piece. He could see that the thirty Doe poems, would, edited, be one poem. He encouraged me to find a home for her to send the poem out.

A great thanks also goes to my writing partner, Tibetha Owen; we have been exchanging work twice a week with a commitment to getting words on the page consistently. She saw the individual Doe pieces as I made my visits to her body day by day. She saw them raw and disjointed and she stayed by my side as they slowly took shape. Tib has an unerring editor's eye: she found duplicated words and overly abundant commas. But more than anything, she always pushed me to be true to the Doe.

My final thanks goes to Adam Booth, a storyteller, musician, teacher and my storytelling coach. He hears symphonies in every word; he taught me how to get words off the page as I pulled all my written pieces about my daughter, Liz, into a one hour storytelling performance. He is a teller who knows how to listen.

He heard every Doe piece week by week and he insisted I keep at it. "This wants to be something," he said. Adam believes in me. He once gave me a card that said, "If you are going to doubt anything, doubt your limitations."

About the Author

Susan Gordon is a storyteller, poet and a prose writer of memoir and fiction. She is a skilled teller of traditional tales and has taught storytelling in colleges, universities and from the barn on her farm. She is now telling personal stories that explore the weave of relationships in her life.

Susan hosts the Hilltop Writers. She has had her work published, been invited to read her poetry at open mics and offers a series of house concerts from her home.

Whether Susan is telling, writing or teaching, her work always invites the listeners to run their fingers across the fabric of their own lives. Susan has a master's degree in narrative therapy and lives with her dog, River, on a 41 acre farm in Ijamsville, Maryland.

www.ingramcontent.com/pod-product-compliance
Lightning Source LLC
Chambersburg PA
CBHW020627300426
44113CB00007B/792